FASHION DESIGNER

Miriam Moss

Crestwood House
New York

FASHION WORLD

FASHION DESIGNER

FASHION MODEL

FASHION PHOTOGRAPHER

STREET FASHION

Library of Congress Cataloging-in-Publication Data

Moss, Miriam.
    Fashion designer by Miriam Moss.—1st Crestwood House ed.
       p. cm.—(Fashion World)

    Summary: Gives a glimpse into the creative world of the fashion designer, showing how new styles are conceived, produced, and marketed

    ISBN 0-89686-610-6

    1. Costume design—Juvenile literature. [1. Costume designers. 2. Costume design. 3. Occupations.] I. Title. II. Series: Moss, Miriam. Fashion world.
TT507.M72 1991
746.9'2—dc20

                                                                                                        90–48323
                                                                                                             CIP
                                                                                                              AC

First Crestwood House edition 1991
Originally published by Wayland (Publishers) Limited,
61 Western Road, Hove, East Sussex, BN3 1JD.
Copyright © 1991 by Wayland (Publishers) Limited

All rights reserved. No part of this book may be reproduced or transmitted in
any form or by any means, electronic or mechanical, including photocopying,
recording, or by any information storage and retrieval system, without
permission in writing from the Publisher.

Macmillan Publishing Company
866 Third Avenue
New York, NY 10022

Printed in Italy
10 9 8 7 6 5 4 3 2 1

CONTENTS

WORKING DESIGNS	4
STARTING UP	6
THE FASHION STUDIO	11
DESIGNER BUSINESS	17
DESIGNER DREAMS	24
GLOSSARY	30
FURTHER READING	31
INDEX	32

CHAPTER ONE
WORKING DESIGNS

"EVERYONE SHOULD dress like a hero." – British fashion designer Katharine Hamnett

Have you ever drawn pictures of clothes that you would like to wear? If you have, then you already know something about the work of the fashion designer. The initial drawings of the fashion designer are translated into patterns. They are then made into finished garments.

Some designers work at the glamorous end of the design business. They create fantastically expensive haute couture outfits for the rich and famous. Others design small quantities of ready-to-wear "designer label" clothes. These are less expensive than haute couture clothes, but the emphasis is still on the quality of the cut and the choice of fabric. Designers also create ready-to-wear clothes in standard sizes for the mass market. They use cheaper materials so that large numbers of garments can be produced at affordable prices.

Fashion designers have to know how clothes and accessories are made. They need to know which materials suit the different styles and seasons. They also need to be in tune with the latest trends and influences. A designer's life may be exciting, but it requires stamina to cope with the pressures of continuous deadlines and long working hours. This book looks at the work of the fashion designer. It takes you behind the scenes of the fashion capitals of the world and reveals, through some of the big names in fashion design, both the exhausting and the exhilarating aspects of the job.

Above: Designs from Next *offer stylish and fashionable clothes for the mass market.*

Opposite: A flamboyant, expensive fashion outfit designed by Katharine Hamnett.

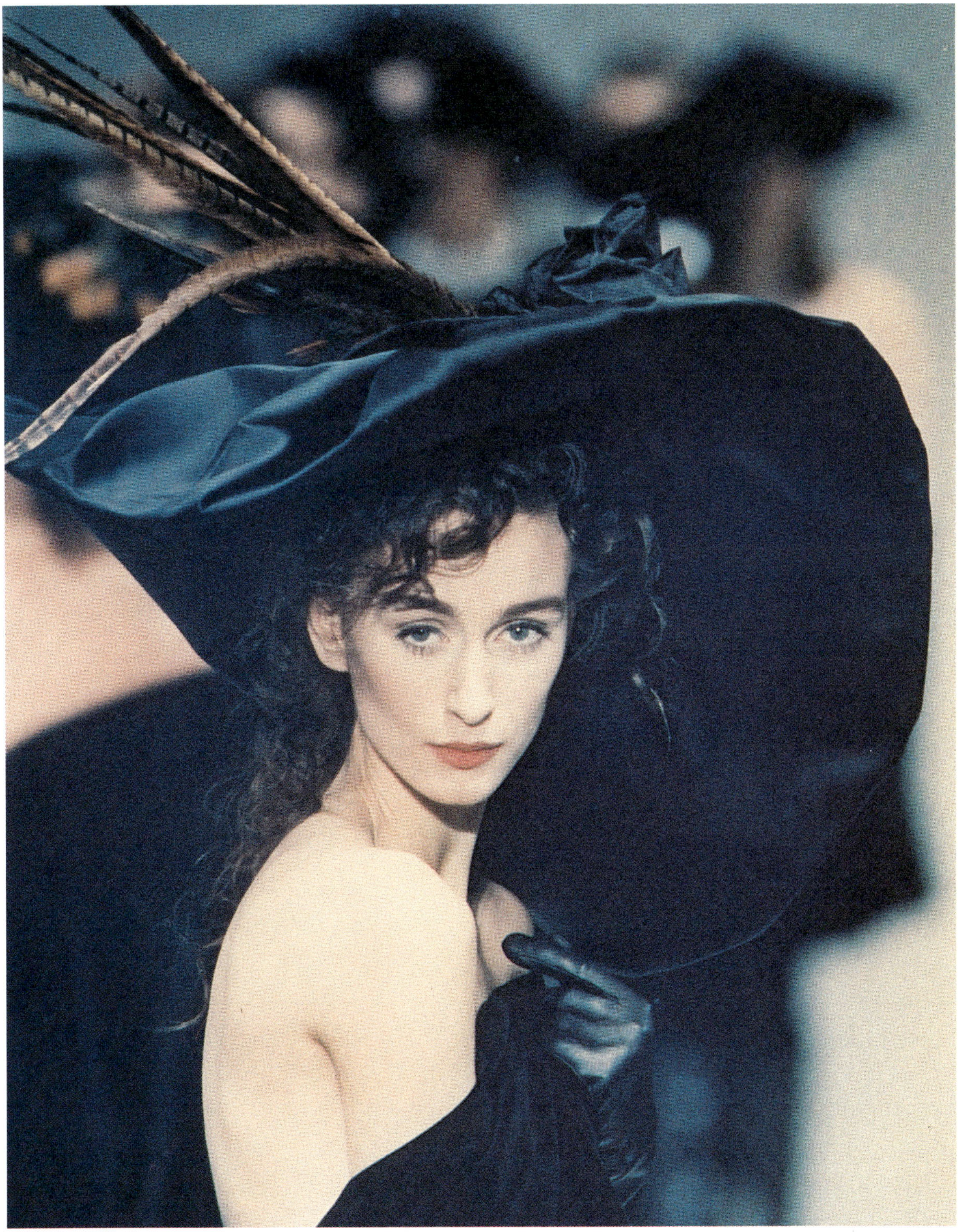

CHAPTER TWO
STARTING UP

"DESIGNING MICKEY Mouse T-shirts . . . that's how I got a taste for fashion and commerce, and everything escalated from there." – Bruce Oldfield

Most people become designers by studying design at school. There they are exposed to the technical and artistic areas of the subject. Students tend to specialize, opting for either women's, men's or children's wear. These three categories are split into other areas. Women's wear, for example, is divided into sportswear, evening wear, lingerie (underwear) and knitwear.

Many college courses include some time in the field, working in the fashion industry. And some offer opportunities to visit fashion houses abroad. Often student courses include internships with an established fashion house. This is a valuable way to make contacts, and students are sometimes offered jobs when they finish their courses. One way for new designers to get exposure is to enter one of the design competitions. In this way college students can show off their designs to those in the trade. These people may then offer them jobs.

Left: These art students have designed their own fabrics, which they have made into lively, original garments.

Above: Finalists show off their clothes in a competition sponsored to find new fashion designers.

Many designers begin their careers working as design assistants. Assistants usually work in the fashion sample rooms alongside pattern makers, sample makers and head designers.

Designers work in three ways. Free-lance designers work for themselves and sell their work to fashion houses, to stores or to clothing manufacturers. Their designs carry each buyer's labels. The second way is to work in-house. This means that designers are employed full-time by fashion companies. Their designs are the property of those companies. Other designers try setting up their own companies. This means they have complete control over their designs, since they are sold under their own labels.

People break into the design business in many different ways. Some experience a lucky break. British designer Richard Torry was just out of school when his work was spotted by the British style guru Malcolm McLaren. Through him Torry met and assisted Britain's famous designer Vivienne Westwood. He was then head-hunted by New York agent Susanne Bartsch, who established Torry in the United States. He now has orders flooding in from leading stores, such as Macy's and Bloomingdale's, and he has started a new label in Japan called London Station.

Not all famous fashion designers have had formal college training. Parisian designer Jean-Paul Gaultier can cut, size, drape, sew and fit clothes with great ease, but he has never attended a fashion school. He says he learned from studying fashion magazines and from working with Pierre Cardin and Michael Goma at the Parisian house of Patou.

Many new designers do not think of starting their own labels until they have spent time

French designer Jean-Paul Gaultier is famous for breaking fashion rules.

Jean-Paul Gaultier sits next to Paloma Picasso, the daughter of the famous painter, at a Paris fashion show.

gaining valuable experience working for other designers. Top American designer Donna Karan went to a fashion school. She became the star apprentice at Anne Klein, then America's top sportswear house. She was appointed company president at 26 and decided to launch her own label. She used Anne Klein's backer, who was prepared to sponsor her $3 million and grant her 50% of the company. It has proved a shrewd investment.

Not all designers, however, start out with design careers in mind. Betty Jackson turned to fashion design after an accident. In her last year at college she was involved in a serious car accident. She was so badly injured that she had to have a leg amputated. She was able to illustrate lying down before she learned to walk again. She says: "With a strong eye for color, style and shape, it seemed a natural progression to channel these qualities into a creative career, and the result was fashion design."

Jackson became an assistant to British designer Wendy Dagworthy who had her own business. Jackson was later approached by Quorum, a company famous in the '60s, which asked her to produce her own collection. She says her time in the elite atmosphere of the Quorum fashion studio taught her a lot about the

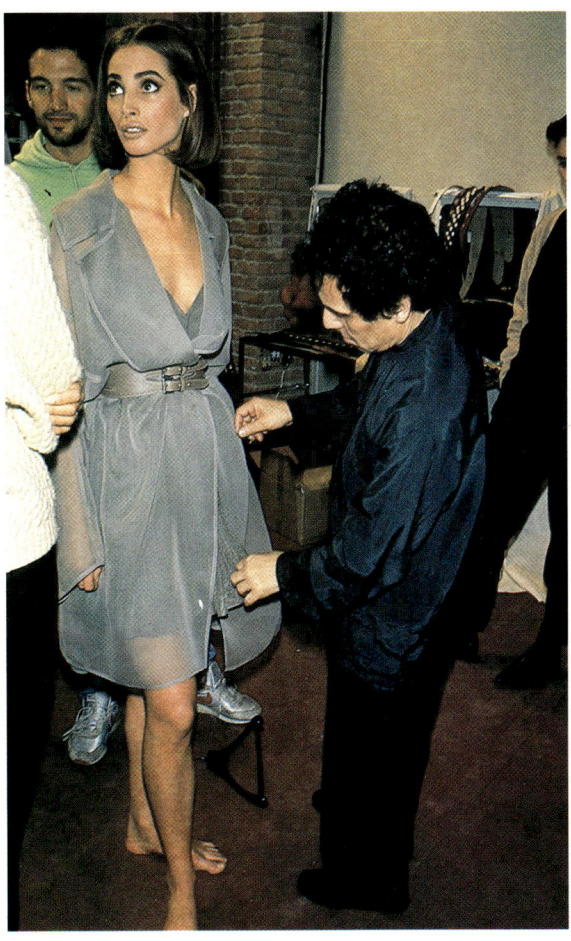

Designer Azzedine Alaïa making final adjustments to one of his creations.

Fashion in the 1970s. From left to right: Paco Rabanne, André Courrèges and Louis Feraud with their models.

fashion industry: "It was when I sorted out what I wanted to do, which area I wanted to go into." In 1981 Jackson started her own company with her husband.

Some people move into fashion design from other careers. An interesting number of successful designers started out as architects. These include Romeo Gigli, Balmain, Courrèges and Azzedine Alaïa. The last has shown his architect's skill by molding his dresses into distinctive body-hugging designs and shapes. Spanish designer Paco Rabanne also changed his career from architect to designer. He says: "It is very important to have access to other ways of creating because all creation is the same gesture. If you can design a dress, you can design a piece of furniture. You have a feel for the technique."

Sometimes a change of heart or a change in circumstances prompts designers to start their own businesses after years in the fashion industry. Graham Knott, along with Richard Frazer, his partner, started the British company Workers for Freedom after 20 years in the fashion industry. He had been an assistant for Valentino in Rome, a college lecturer and a merchandising manager for Liberty's of London. There, he grew tired of climbing the executive ladder. "It meant taking my earring out and wearing suits. Workers for Freedom was started as a result of my identity crisis!"

CHAPTER THREE
THE FASHION STUDIO

"SOMETIMES YOU rack your brains for the muse to strike and she doesn't and you get in a panic thinking you'll never think of anything again." – Betty Jackson

Fashion design is as much about producing and selling designs as it is about creating them. Many people imagine that the leading fashion designers sit around all day sketching fantastic designs that are immediately whisked off and created by their team. In fact, fashion designing is mainly a production job that involves meeting deadlines, budgeting, coping under stress and working very long hours.

Negotiating budgets and deadlines for fashion designs from a Hanae Mori collection in Tokyo.

Design teams develop a range of clothes for a number of seasons each year. Designers have to work about a year in advance so that their designs reach the stores on time. As soon as one collection, or range of clothes, is completed, they start on the next one. Each collection is carefully planned, and a theme is often used to provide inspiration. A team is headed by the fashion designer, who designs the shape and style of each garment. Another team member is the knitwear designer, who works out color combinations and patterns. Then there is the fabric designer, who designs fabrics for the fashion designer. Finally there are assistants, sample makers and pattern makers.

Designers have different methods of working. They might sketch their ideas on paper. Or they might work directly with the fabric itself. They drape it on a dress form, folding and tucking until the right shape emerges. Other designers adapt patterns from previous collections.

A number of design elements have to be considered, particularly in a commercial fashion studio that produces designs for the mass market. The design team needs to have a clear idea of the market that the garments are being made for. And they need to decide for which season they will be suitable. The cost of production also has to be sorted out. This includes the cost of the fabrics used and any trimmings, such as buttons, zippers or lace.

When everyone is satisfied with a design, the designer usually makes a paper pattern. If the design is for a dress, for example, the sample maker makes a trial version from a plain-colored material such as muslin. This is called a toile. The toile is put on a dress form where any alterations are made. When the designer is

Opposite: Surrounded by rolls of fabric and aided by his model, tailor and assistants, Yves Saint Laurent examines the effect of his design.

Below: A woolen outfit from Pierre Balmain's autumn/winter collection.

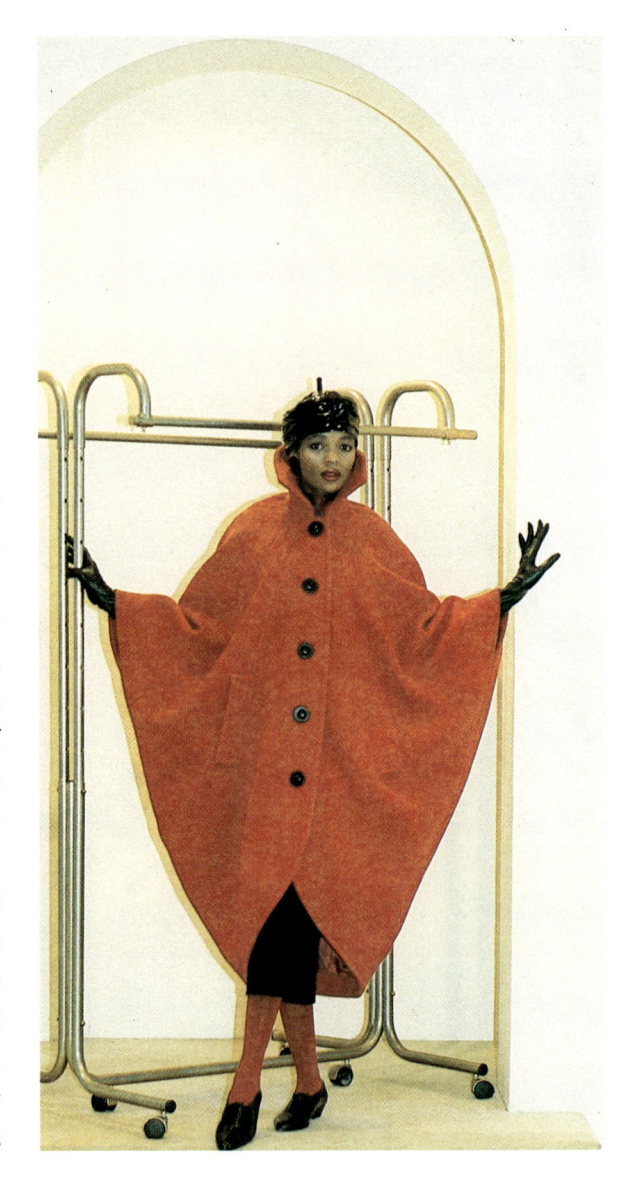

happy with the shape, the toile is given to a professional pattern cutter, who makes an accurate working pattern out of cardboard. Finally a sample garment is made up in the chosen fabric. One garment may be produced in several different colors. The result might be an exclusive haute couture dress worth $65,000, a designer label dress worth $300 or a mass-produced dress for $65.

THE COLLECTION

Betty Jackson designs five collections a year. She explains how a collection happens: "It's terribly simple and logical, really. We look at fabrics, choose colors and then work on shape. Collections develop. We don't reject what has gone before. Obviously you have to make sure that you have the basics in any collection, the clothes that good department stores are going to buy." The pressures inside the fashion studio are great. Says Betty Jackson: "There's never enough time. A lot of things are done on the spur of the moment on the back of envelopes, because there is a problem in production or somewhere else. But often they are the things that work best!"

Since designers often have to create collections from thin air, they need inspiration. One of French designer Jean Louis Scherrer's shows was inspired by a trip to Rajasthan in

British designer Arabella Pollen discusses the designs for her latest collection with her cutter.

India. The show included swirling pants suits, jeweled turbans and spicy-colored silks. British jewelry designer Dinny Hall says she is inspired by classical forms: "I'm heavily into symbols, and I love domes and spirals."

In his 20 years in fashion, French designer Jean-Paul Gaultier has been inspired by a wide range of ideas. His creations have ranged from clothes that look like nuns' habits to skeletal style T-shirts and raincoats with X-ray prints of spinal columns and rib cages. This developed because he was "interested in the interior of people. And what could be more intimate than an X ray?" American designer Geoffrey Beene is inspired by extravagant mixes of clashing patterns. Isaac Mizrahi has created clothes with op art graphics inspired, he says, "by the naive art of Matisse."

Soviet designer Irina Burmistrova turns to unusual materials for her inspiration. Her designs include bows made from salvaged black plastic, gray foam with serrated edges, black and green plastic garbage bags and bracelets made from rubberized cable. She dismisses the lack of ordinary materials in her designs by saying: "I am more interested in finding a new form, a new way of expressing art through clothes."

The relationship between fashion and other art forms is complicated, but it can be very revealing. Movie director Wim Wenders made a film about the designer Yohji Yamamoto at work. The movie explores the inside of the fashion studio. The images show the workroom team clustered around the hem of a dress, pinning, tucking and sewing, while others measure on the cutting table or coax a fabric into shape. Meanwhile Yohji Yamamoto, pincushion on his wrist, modifies a design by slashing off a sleeve.

Left: A classical look is achieved with these two designs from a Hardy Amies spring collection for men.

Above: What do you think inspired Gianni Versace to create these outfits for his spring collection?

Above: Yohji Yamamoto being applauded by his models at the end of a Paris show.

A wonderfully simple, stylish design by Romeo Gigli.

German-born Karl Lagerfeld describes how he designs: "Making a jacket with shoulder pads is easy, like dressing a Christmas tree – you just hang the fabric from them. Without shoulder pads, you're building on air."

Katharine Hamnett explains the difficulties of describing exactly what a designer does: "It's hard to talk about clothes. A collar is all wrong and you cut a few inches off and it's right. How can you explain that? Before he looked like a nerd, now he looks like some wonderful '50s American good guy, a prince, a wag."

Colleagues of Italian designer Romeo Gigli say that when he is at work on a collection, he is like a man possessed. He often stays at his drawing board until three or four o'clock in the morning, poring over jewelry samples from exotic parts of the world, selecting fabrics and continually pacing back and forth. He explains: "Everything can give an emotion: a fork, a star, a medieval painting. For me, these emotions are transmitted onto paper in the form of a garment that has a place in daily life."

CHAPTER FOUR

DESIGNER BUSINESS

"MY FIRST attempts at designing and creating were for friends. The next step was being approached by a store to do a small collection and eventually gaining enough resources to design my own collection and start my own company." – Wendy Dagworthy

THE SHOW

Fashion shows are where buyers come from all over the world to view the completed collections and talk about colors, delivery dates and prices. The French collections, for example, take place in Paris over a ten-day period. There are over 40 shows. Every six months the fashion editors from magazines such as *Vogue* and *Elle* – and journalists from the *New York Times* and the *International Herald Tribune* – arrive. Buyers and the elegantly rich (who do not balk at paying $3,000 for an Armani, Ungaro or Valentino suit) also come. The ready-to-wear colections can be seen in the halls of Paris's Louvre museum, although not all the designers show their collections in these elegant surroundings. Some collections are shown in tents on the banks of the Seine. Other collections are shown in more unusual surroundings: Jean-Paul Gaultier's assistant once used an abandoned bomb shelter in the southeast district of Paris.

Behind the scenes, models squeeze themselves into body-molded Azzedine Alaïa dresses with slashed sides. Or they wear outfits that trail out yards of wildly colored silk. The atmosphere is electric. Wim Wenders describes the atmosphere before one of

Compare these Yohji Yamamoto designs with those on the opposite page: Different themes radically change the color and style of a collection.

Yamamoto's runway shows: "It was very tense – like being backstage in a theater on the first night of a play."

Fashion shows do not stop at merely showing clothes. They are an experience. Jean-Paul Gaultier has incorporated Buddhist prayers and Gregorian chants. The clothes in one of Rifat Ozbek's summer collections were all white and featured a New Age couple cradling the popular accessory of the 1990s – a baby.

Designers might get their message across by using loud rock music and raunchy, aggressive dancing. Or they have models appearing in plumes of smoke from holes beneath the runway. Yamamoto's twice-yearly shows are famous for his pioneering method of presentation. His models march down the runway in military formation, never standing still. The lighting, props and accessories are all carefully chosen to give an overall look that complements the theme. The models add their own touches by either appearing dignified and aloof, or overflowing with rebellion – even sticking their tongues out at the audience.

THE FASHION CAPITALS

The busy fashion year includes many major events for designers. One of these is the fabric exhibition at the Interstoff Clothing Textiles Trade fair in Frankfurt, Germany, in April and October. Here new colors are predicted two years ahead. The children's wear collections are

Opposite: A shot showing fun on the runway during a recent fashion event.

Above: Models showing very specific silhouettes with these designs by Claude Montana.

British designer Zandra Rhodes is famous for her brilliant, unusual evening wear.

shown in Florence in June and in Paris in September. On top of this, there is the constant round of international designer and ready-to-wear collections in the different fashion capitals.

Each fashion capital has its own individual style. In Milan making money from making people look good is *the* industry. Fashion addicts love the sleek sophistication of Italian clothing by Giorgio Armani, Gianfranco Ferre, Gianni Versace and Valentino, as well as designs from large manufacturers such as Benetton.

London's best designers tend to be anti-establishment. Vivienne Westwood, for example, is considered by some to be Britain's fashion visionary. The image is of young, innovative fashion, and resisting conformity is one of London's strengths. As Jean-Paul Gaultier says: "The English are so energizing because they have no fashion barriers."

Fashion in New York City is led by multimillionaires such as Ralph Lauren and Calvin Klein, along with Geoffrey Beene, Donna Karan and Oscar de la Renta. The American fashion capital took off with the sporting look and has not looked back. The clothes are clean cut, direct and wearable – famous for their dressed-down chic. Other American designers, such as Bob Mackie, provide a less serious fashion style. He specializes in beads and sequins that drip down the backs of silk dresses. He is famous for his sequined wet suits as well as for the skimpy, gossamer outfits he makes for Tina Turner and Cher. He says he makes his dresses for performers. The dresses "look like butterfly wings – but they have to be made like iron."

In New York City, Christian Lacroix may sell only about a hundred of his new designs to

Left: Designer Christian Lacroix is persuaded to accompany one of his models down the runway.

Below: Singers such as Whitney Houston are always looking for chic, eye-catching outfits.

private customers each season. Chanel, Christian Dior, Ungaro, Givenchy and other French fashion houses pack their Paris samples in trunks and ship them to New York for American clients. Many designers send videos to their clients throughout the world. As well as these outlets, top designers need stores. The showcase sights are on New York's Fifth Avenue, London's Bond Street or the Boulevard Saint Germain in Paris. When someone has walked into a shop, bought the clothes and looks great in them, the cycle is complete. Betty Jackson says: "I like seeing people in the street wearing my clothes. It's the biggest thrill you can imagine. Better than any press write-up."

A Jasper Conran design being modeled at a fashion show held in grand surroundings.

DESIGNER RANGES

The running of a designer business needs a shrewd financial plan and a cool head. When a fashion company has established regular orders from buyers, the company will often want to expand into another area of the fashion industry. To do this, the company will need money. Finding financial backing is a major stumbling block for young designers. If a company does not have enough money to expand, it may grant a license to a clothing manufacturer to use the designer label in return for a fixed fee.

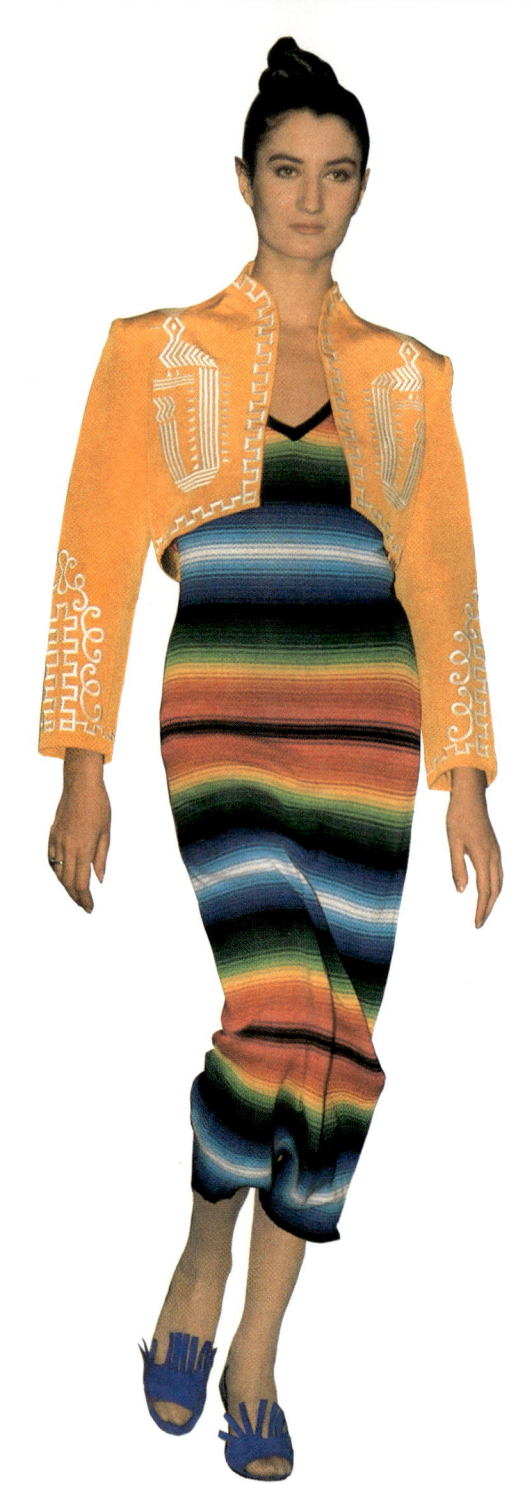

Clothes designed by Rifat Ozbek are famous for their motifs and bright colors.

British designer Jasper Conran explains what happens to the average designer: "You start off with no money and you do well. That is about the worst thing that can happen. You sell about $100,000 of clothes in your first season and need to find $50,000 to make them. The next season you get orders for $200,000 and you get hit by a production problem or by a boutique that doesn't pay its bills. Just as you're doing well, you are virtually bankrupt. This is when the magical backer comes along."

Designing as a business has an international flavor. For example, French designer Jean-Paul Gaultier is financed by Japanese capital and manufactures his clothes in Italy. At Christian Dior, the French house, the collections are designed by Ferre, an Italian. German designer Jil Sander has her art direction done by Frenchman Marc Ascoli and her advertising done by Spanish photographer Javicr Vallhonrat.

Designer clothes may be wonderful, but their cost puts them beyond the range of most people. Realizing this, many designers produce designs in several price ranges, offering two-level or even three-level collections. These have the same designer trademark, but with careful economies in fabric and cut. They are sold at less expensive prices. American designer Ralph Lauren has always offered several levels of style, but Yves Saint Laurent was the first Parisian designer to realize the potential of a variety of price ranges. He initially launched an accessory collection that led into the YSL Variation line. This echoes his haute couture look but at a third of the price.

Karl Lagerfeld is the latest big name in Paris to launch a cheaper line. He has created high-quality tailoring with exaggerated detail in his less expensive KL label. Giorgio Armani, famous for his streamlined tailoring, has three labels. The least expensive is called Emporio. In Great Britain, Workers for Freedom, famous for its softly styled separates in natural fabrics, has a subsidiary line simply called White. Irish designer Paul Costello creates a classically European style with the use of pure Irish linen, but he also has a less expensive line called Dressage.

A Calvin Klein outfit showing the appeal of stylish designs at affordable prices.

CHAPTER FIVE

DESIGNER DREAMS

"I DON'T copy, I digest. Most of all, I dare!" – **Jean-Paul Gaultier**

Whether it is through the creative touch of Yohji Yamamoto, the originality of John Galliano, the humor of Vivienne Westwood or the street-modern style of Rifat Ozbek, top designers display a remarkable range of images. These ideas usually begin as tiny germs. Today's designers are constantly looking for new inspirations into the future so that their designs will inspire us – but are there any rules to designing?

French fashion designer Jean-Paul Gaultier says: "I design *without* rules. I'm successful because my designs have more to do with the way they are combined than with the clothes themselves." He continues: "I work like a fashion editor. I assemble the elements. Mixing elements is the base of my style. For example, I've put flea-market sweaters, ski pants and riding boots all together."

Giorgio Armani's fierce fashion rules are reflected in the clothes and shoes he likes to wear himself.

Vivienne Westwood's zest for life comes across both in her public image and in her often eccentric designs.

A lot of designers have quite fixed ideas about fashion and style. Yohji Yamamoto goes so far as to say: "I don't need color. It brings out emotions that bother me a lot." He continues: "Human beings are not beautiful when they're symmetrical. If you are human, you cannot make perfect things; when I make something symmetrical, I want to break it, to destroy it a little." He says: "When you are honest and skillful and put emotion into your work, a product is 'given' to you. When I see something that is made by me, I see it as a natural happening."

Giorgio Armani's designing laws are very detailed. He will not tolerate high heels. He also maintains you can wear buttons or earrings but never both. His polished fashions are reflected in the strict rules he lays down for the staff in his restored seventeenth-century palazzo in Milan that is the brain center of his $50 million fashion empire. No one is allowed to wear dark stockings, nail polish or high heels. British designer Joseph Ettedgui, on the other hand, believes that to be a successful designer, you need a fluid approach. He hates anything that is overplanned.

Some of the most innovative designers have had to make very strong statements to get their new ideas across to the public. Italian designer Romeo Gigli felt he had to be extreme to get away from what he hated in Italian fashion:

"Big, ugly fur coats and spike heels that make women totter. And I hate a constricted dress that holds the body in like a harness." He caused great consternation at first with his plainly dressed, pale, innocent-looking models in muddied colors and flat shoes.

Success for a designer often means standing alone. People at Workers for Freedom explain: "We started out four years ago, doing what we wanted, and we've stuck with it. It's been a learning process, but we've tried to maintain this independent attitude. We want our customers to look different without looking retro or ridiculous."

Some designers are well aware of their reputations as innovators. One of Britain's best-known designers of radical chic is Vivienne Westwood. She is the creator of the Mini Crinnie, the tube skirt and pirate shirt, and she was responsible for the punk rock outbreak and New Romantic fashion in the 1980s. Her twice-yearly fashion shows are crowded with people from the fashion world eager to see her newest departure. She says of herself: "I am an innovator – maybe it's arrogant, but I know it's the truth."

DESIGNER LIFE-STYLES

Making a lot of money out of designing brings its own stresses, but not all fashion designers are there for the money. The Tunisian Azzedine Alaïa is a huge Parisian success with a top reputation, but he shuns the mega-star image. He is profoundly shy of the media and keeps himself out of the public eye. He seems to live for fashion and not fame, working constantly and seeing only very few close friends.

His success can be judged by the fact that the art directors, the national press and buyers are prepared to fly back to Paris just to see his collection three weeks after the other collections have been shown. He also has a devoted following of top models who travel from all over the world at their own expense to model his collection free, just so they can have one of his dresses. Alaïa is known for his silhouettes that

The cost of Yves Saint Laurent's enormous fame is his increasing isolation.

Designer Karl Lagerfeld poses with a model after presenting the Chanel collection in Paris.

are combined with fine finishing and rich, off-beat colors that create a simple, sophisticated look.

Designers avoid publicity and the glamorous life-style in different ways. Some become legendary recluses who appear sadly isolated by their creativity. A member of Yves Saint Laurent's staff says: "Yves is a recluse. He lives alone with his staff – a chauffeur, a butler, a bodyguard and his dog. He sees people one by one. The only place you ever see him outside his studio is backstage at the show, and no one who doesn't work with him is allowed there."

Betty Jackson puts designing clothes into perspective: "Clothes are certainly not the most important thing in the world to me, but they do enable me to live. I think it's a very dangerous thing to get too serious about it. It's easy to get caught up in the glamorous, shallow side of the fashion world. Luckily I have been able to siphon off the bits that I want to be involved with." British designer Joseph Ettedgui says he keeps a sense of perspective by listening to people who are not living fashion as he is. And Romeo Gigli manages to cope with the pressures of his work by returning to India and Morocco "for the philosophy of life, the quiet and the sun." He says: "I regard fashion as a vocation, not as a career. I do not let work control my life." He adds: "My clothes are for the women I would like to meet."

Donna Karan has the fastest-growing design business in New York City. She puts the secret of her success down to her fashion method, which she calls the "capsule wardrobe." The foundation is the bodysuit, and over this she adds an interchangeable line of separates in luxurious but unfussy fabrics. She has mastered the look of understated chic. "My clothes are not fantasy fashion dreamed up in an ivory tower," she says. "I see what is missing from my closet and I design it."

Gabriella Forte, vice-president of Giorgio Armani's corporation, explains Armani's enormously successful formula: "Every decision goes back to him so the product has a clarity. What I am doing today I only do because he thought about it five years ago."

Designers have to be skilled at coming up with designs that have continual appeal. Nicole Farhi maintains that her clothes remain popular because she is "doing the same as 20 years ago."

WEAR NEXT

What about the future? What are the designer dreams for the 1990s? Fashion public relations expert Lynne Franks says: "It's a designer's job to reflect the mood around." Fashion is highly sensitive to changes in attitudes. The concerns of the 1980s were with money, power and ourselves. The New Age dressing of the 1990s points to a greater concern with spiritual things – with purity, simplicity and comfort, and designers are bringing us a gentler and more relaxed image. This is Workers for Freedom's prediction of the clothes it will be making for the 1990s: "Clothes that make you feel special without making you feel weird."

John Galliano has already put his dreams about the next century's clothes on paper. His fashion victim in 2010 wears a bodysuit made from fabric that reacts to light and temperature. "Fabrics that react to light, to earth or body temperature will lead to protective designer clothing. This could be in the form of fabrics whose structures and color react to the elements." He dreams of a light-sensitive fabric that can insulate or cool according to temperatures so that it can be worn all year. He says: "Imagine wearing a midnight blue jumpsuit in winter that breathes and cools in summer after turning white?"

Galliano maintains that fashion is a sensuous experience. "Wearing clothes is part of our touching and feeling senses, like smell and taste." His view is not so strange if we think about the way the structure of materials has developed. We now wear fabrics that mix synthetics with pure wools. This means we have tailored suits that stretch with the wearer, do not crease and have long-lasting properties.

Designers have a lot in store for us. As Ralph Lauren says: "The goal is still quality – and that does not mean boring, any more than classic means dowdy."

Opposite: Designer hats for both men and women are big business at the Ascot races in Great Britain.

Above: The extraordinary top by Thierry Mugler shows just how adventurous designs can be.

GLOSSARY

Anti-establishment Against authority.
Couturier A person who designs, makes and sells fashion clothes.
Designer label clothes Well-made garments produced in small quantities.
Fashion house An established fashion design company.
Fashion victim Colloquial expression for someone who goes along with the latest fashions.
Gossamer A fabric of the very finest texture.
Haute couture French for fine tailoring. A garment made for an individual customer.
Insulate To prevent heat or cold from escaping.
Internship Temporary employment generally arranged by a school.

Mini Crinnie Short, full skirt worn over layers of petticoats.
New Age fashion Fashion of the 1990s with emphasis on white, flowing shapes and fabrics.
New Romantic fashion Flamboyant 1980s fashion.
Op art Short for optical art. Art that includes contrasting shapes and colors that challenge and sometimes confuse the eye.
Palazzo Italian for palace.
Serrated Having a notched or sawlike edge.
Silhouette The outline of a figure.
Siphon To draw off.
Toile A trial version of a garment.

FURTHER READING

Bolognese, Don & Raphael, Elaine. *Drawing Fashions: Figures, Faces & Techniques*. New York: Franklin Watts, 1985.

Boucher, Francois. *Twenty Thousand Years of Fashion: The History of Costume and Personal Adornment*. New York: Abrams, 1987.

Cantwell, Lois. *Modeling*. New York: Franklin Watts, 1986.

Colquitt, Ken. *Modeling Made Easy: Getting Started Without Getting Taken*. Atlanta, GA: Starmakers, 1988.

Hodgman, Ann. *A Day in the Life of a Fashion Designer*. Mahwah, NJ: Troll Associates, 1987.

Lasch, Judith. *The Teen Model Book*. Englewood Cliffs, NJ: Julian Messner, 1985.

MacGil, Gillis. *Your Future as a Model*. New York: Rosen, 1982.

Slade, Richard. *Your Book of Modeling*. Albuquerque, NM: Transatlantic, 1968.

Weinstein, Robert. *Breaking into Modeling*. New York: Arco, 1983.

ACKNOWLEDGMENTS

The Publisher would like to thank the following agencies and photographers used in this book: Camera Press 4 (Sean Cunningham), 16, 20 (C. Sagoe), 21 (Ben Coster); Sara Leigh Lewis 9, 12, 29; London Features International 22 (Cyndi Loper), 25 (Andy Catlin); Rex Features 6 (Sichov), 8 (Siph Press), 13 (left, Sylvan Mason), 14 (Ian Turner), 15 (Nils Jorgensen), 18 (Dixon), 30 (Butler); Frank Spooner 19 (Edelhajt Winczewski); Storm Model Agency 11; Topham Picture Source 5, 13 (right); David Trainer 17.

INDEX

Numbers that appear in **bold** refer to captions.

Alaïa, Azzedine   **9**, 10, 17, 26
Amies, Hardy   **15**
Armani, Giorgio   17, 20, 23, **24**, 25, 28

Balmain, Pierre   10, **12**
Beene, Geoffrey   14, 20
Benetton   20
Britain   8, 9, 14, 20, 21, 23, 27, **29**
Burmistrova, Irina   14
Buyer   8, 17, 22

Chanel   21, **27**
Classic designs   **15**, 28
Clothing manufacturers   8
Collections   **11**, 12, 13, **14**, **15**, 17, 20
Conran, Jasper   **22**, 23
Costello, Paul   23
Courrèges, André   10, **10**

Dagworthy, Wendy   9, 17
Deadlines   4, 11, 17
de la Renta, Oscar   20
Designer label   4, 13, 22
Dior, Christian   21, 23

Emporio   23

Farhi, Nicole   28
Fashion
  capitals   4, 18–23
  houses   6, 8, 10, 22
  industry   6, 22
  magazines   8, 17
  seasons   4, 12, **15**, 28
  school   6, **7**, 9
  shows   9, 13, **16**, 17, 18, **22**
Feraud, Louis   **10**
Ferre, Gianfranco   20, 23
Financial backing   22
France   13, 14, 17, 21, 23, 24
Free-lance designers   8

Galliano, John   24, 28
Gaultier, Jean-Paul   8, **8**, **9**, 14, 17, 18, 20, 23, 24
Germany   16, 18, 23
Gigli, Romeo   10, 16, **16**, 25, 27
Givenchy   21

Hamnett, Katharine   4, **4**, 16
Haute couture   4, 13

Italy   10, 16, 20, 23, 25

Jackson, Betty   9, 11, 13, 21, 27
Japan   8, **11**, 23

Karan, Donna   9, 20, 27
Klein, Anne   9
Klein, Calvin   20, **23**

Lacroix, Christian   20, **21**
Lagerfeld, Karl   16, 23, **27**
Lauren, Ralph   20, 23, 28

Mass market   4, 12
McLaren, Malcolm   8
Mizrahi, Isaac   14
Montana, Claude   **19**

Mugler, Thierry   **29**

New Age fashions   18, 28
New Romantic fashions   26
Next   **4**

Oldfield, Bruce   6
Ozbek, Rifat   18, **22**, 24

Pattern makers   8, 12, 13
Pollen, Arabella   **14**

Rabanne, Paco   10, **10**
Rhodes, Zandra   20

Saint Laurent, Yves   12, 23, **26**, 27
Scherrer, Jean Louis   13
Sportswear   9

Toile   12, 13

Ungaro   17, 21
United States   8, 9, 14, 16, 20, 21, 23

Valentino   10, 17, 20
Versace, Gianni   **15**, 20

Westwood, Vivienne   8, 20, 24, **25**, 26
White   23
Workers for Freedon   10, 23, 26, 28

Yamamoto, Yohji   14, **16**, **17**, 18, 24, 25